On your 60th
Love from
Your Sister Betty

THE

LAKELAND POETS

AN ILLUSTRATED
Collection

Photographs by **ROB TALBOT**

Compiled by JENNY WILSON

WEIDENFELD & NICOLSON · London

Words and pictures in this form
© GEORGE WEIDENFELD & NICOLSON, 1991

Photographs © TALBOT-WHITEMAN, 1991

Design by PETER BRIDGEWATER

First published in Great Britain by
WEIDENFELD AND NICOLSON LTD,
91 Clapham High Street,
London SW4 7TA

British Library Cataloguing in Publication Data
The Lakeland Poets— An Illustrated Collection
1. Cumbria (England). English poetry
I. Wilson, Jenny
821.008032

ISBN 0 297 83121 6

Phototypeset by Keyspools Ltd, Golborne, Lancs
Printed and Bound in Italy

CONTENTS

P R E F A C E

There is one corner of England that will, it seems, remain unspoiled for ever. 'When first I made/once more the circuit of our little Lake/if ever happiness hath lodg'd with man,/that day consummate happiness was mine'. So wrote Wordsworth over one hundred years ago, and today any visitor to the Lake District might feel the same. It is undoubtedly a place of outstanding beauty and dramatic splendour.

With its powerful waterfalls, famed serene lakes, majestic mountains, tarns, rivers, fells and meadowland, it is no surprise that it has long been a place of pilgrimage for writers and artists. Wordsworth, his sister Dorothy, and Coleridge made their home at Dove Cottage in Grasmere. John Ruskin lived at Brantwood, with a perfect view of Coniston Water. Coleridge's son Hartley and Thomas de Quincey both lived at Nab Cottage on the banks of Rydal Water. Keats, Shelley and Tennyson were all enchanted by the haunting beauty of the Lakeland scenery, which was perfectly in tune with the sensibility of the new Romantic movement. It seemed tailor-made to inspire an appreciative awareness of one's surroundings, visions of happy tranquillity, awe at the wilder reaches of the peaks. Here could be found Wordsworth's unforgettable 'host of daffodils', Coleridge's 'varied scene/of wood, hill, dale, and sparkling brook between', Keats' 'voice of waters'.

The poems have been divided into four sections, each section itself a division of time: the hours of the day, the seasons of the year, the ages of man, and the more general scan of life and the after-life. Each section reflects some of the central preoccupations of the Romantic Lakeland poets: the joys and tribulations of day to day life, a love of nature, the sublime and the beautiful, the nature of existence itself. The poems are matched with evocative photographs of the area taken by Rob Talbot over the course of a year, and paintings by contemporary artists. Together, the poems and pictures stand testimony to Dorothy Wordsworth's words in her *Journals*— 'a place made for all kinds of beautiful works of art and nature.'

SUNRISE
TO
SUNSET

CHILL'D BY the night, the drooping
  Rose of May
Mourns the long absence of the
  lovely Day;
Young Day returning at her
  promis'd hour
Weeps o'er the sorrows of her
  favourite Flower.

≈ COLERIDGE

TO HOPE

Now MORNING from her orient chamber came,
    And her first footsteps touch'd a verdant hill:
    Crowning its lawny crest with amber flame,
    Silv'ring the untainted gushes of its rill;
    Which, pure from mossy beds, did down distil,
    And after parting beds of simple flowers,
    By many streams a little lake did fill,
    Which round its marge reflected woven bowers,
    And, in its middle space, a sky that never lowers.

——— *0* ———

[J O H N K E A T S]

From LINES ON AN AUTUMNAL EVENING

*D*EAR NATIVE BROOK! like PEACE, so placidly
Smoothing through fertile fields thy current meek!
Dear native brook! where first young POESY
Stared wildly-eager in her noontide dream!
Where BLAMELESS PLEASURES dimple QUIET's cheek,
As water-lilies ripple a slow stream!
Dear native haunts! where Virtue still is gay,
Where Friendship's fix'd-star sheds a mellow'd ray;
Where LOVE a crown of thornless Roses wears:
Where soften'd SORROW smiles within her tears;
And Mem'ry, with a VESTAL's chaste employ,
Unceasing feeds the lambent flame of Joy!
No more your skylarks melting from the sight
Shall thrill the attuned heart-string with delight:—
No more shall deck your pensive Pleasures sweet
With wreaths of sober hue my evening seat.
Yet dear to Fancy's eye your varied scene
Of wood, hill, dale, and sparkling brook between!
Yet sweet to Fancy's ear the warbled song,
That soars on Morning's wing your vales among.

SCENES OF MY HOPE! the aking eye ye leave
Like yon bright hues that paint the clouds of eve!
Tearful and sad'ning with the sadden'd blaze
Mine eye the gleam pursues with wistful gaze:
Sees shades on shades with deeper tint impend,
Till chill and damp the moonless night descend.

———— *o* ————

[SAMUEL TAYLOR COLERIDGE]

WRITTEN ON THE BANKS OF
WASTWATER DURING A CALM

*I*s this the lake, the cradle of the storms,
Where silence never tames the mountain-roar,
Where poets fear their self-created forms,
Or sunk in trance severe, their God adore?
Is this the Lake, for ever dark and loud
With wave and tempest, cataract and cloud?
Wondrous, O Nature! is thy sovereign power,
That gives to horror hours of peaceful mirth;
For here might beauty build her summer-bower!
Lo! where yon rainbow spans the smiling earth,
And, clothed in glory, through a silent shower
The mighty Sun comes forth, a godlike birth;
While, 'neath his loving eye, the gentle Lake
Lies like a sleeping child too blest to wake!

——— *o* ———

[JOHN WILSON]

'HOW MANY BARDS GILD THE LAPSES OF TIME!'

*H*OW MANY BARDS gild the lapses of time!
A few of them have ever been the food
Of my delighted fancy, — I could brood
Over their beauties, earthly, or sublime:
And often, when I sit me down to rhyme,
These will in throngs before my mind intrude:
But no confusion, no disturbance rude
Do they occasion; 'tis a pleasing chime.
So the unnumber'd sounds that evening store;
The songs of birds — the whispering of the leaves —
The voice of waters — the great bell that heaves
With solemn sound, — and thousand others more,
That distance of recognizance bereaves,
Make pleasing music, and not wild uproar.

—————— o ——————

[JOHN KEATS]

From THE PRELUDE, BOOK IV

W HEN FIRST I MADE
    Once more the circuit of our little Lake
    If ever happiness hath lodg'd with man,
    That day consummate happiness was mine,
    Wide-spreading, steady, calm, contemplative.
    The sun was set, or setting, when I left
    Our cottage door, and evening soon brought on
    A sober hour, not winning or serene,
    For cold and raw the air was, and untun'd;
    But, as a face we love is sweetest then
    When sorrow damps it, or, whatever look
    It chance to wear is sweetest if the heart
    Have fulness in itself, even so with me
    It fared that evening. Gently did my soul
    Put off her veil, and, self-transmuted, stood
    Naked as in the presence of her God.
    As on I walked, a comfort seem'd to touch
    A heart that had not been disconsolate,
    Strength came where weakness was not known to be,
    At least not felt; and restoration came,
    Like an intruder, knocking at the door
    Of unacknowledg'd weariness.

——— *o* ———

[WILLIAM WORDSWORTH]

From EPIPSYCHIDION

O NE STOOD on my path who seemed
  As like the glorious shape which I had dreamed,
  As is the Moon, whose changes ever run
  Into themselves, to the eternal Sun;
  The cold chaste Moon, the Queen of Heaven's bright isles,
  Who makes all beautiful on which she smiles;
  That wandering shrine of soft yet icy flame
  Which ever is transformed, yet still the same,
  And warms not but illumines. Young and fair
  As the descended Spirit of that sphere,
  She hid me, as the Moon may hide the night
  From its own darkness, until all was bright
  Between the Heaven and Earth of my calm mind,
  And, as a cloud charioted by the wind,
  She led me to a cave in that wild place,
  And sate beside me, with her downward face
  Illumining my slumbers, like the Moon
  Waxing and waning o'er Endymion.

And I was laid asleep, spirit and limb,
And all my being became bright or dim
As the Moon's image in a summer sea,
According as she smiled or frowned on me;
And there I lay, within a chaste cold bed:
Alas, I then was nor alive nor dead:—
For at her silver voice came Death and Life,
Unmindful each of their accustomed strife,
Masked like twin babes, a sister and a brother,
The wandering hopes of one abandoned mother,
And through the cavern without wings they flew,
And cried 'Away, he is not of our crew.'
I wept, and though it be a dream, I weep.

WHAT STORMS then shook the ocean of my sleep,
Blotting that Moon, whose pale and waning lips
Then shrank as in the sickness of eclipse;—
And how my soul was as a lampless sea,
And who was then its Tempest; and when She,
The Planet of that hour, was quenched, what frost
Crept o'er those waters, till from coast to coast
The moving billows of my being fell
Into a death of ice, immoveable;—
And then—what earthquakes made it gape and split,
The white Moon smiling all the while on it,
These words conceal:—if not, each word would be
The key of staunchless tears. Weep not for me!

——— *0* ———

[PERCY BYSSHE SHELLEY]

T O   S L E E P

O SOFT EMBALMER of the still midnight!
   Shutting, with careful fingers and benign,
   Our gloom-pleased eyes, embower'd from the light,
   Enshaded in forgetfulness divine;
   O soothest Sleep! if so it please thee, close,
   In midst of this thine hymn, my willing eyes,
   Or wait the amen, ere thy poppy throws
   Around my bed its lulling charities;
   Then save me, or the passèd day will shine
   Upon my pillow, breeding many woes;
   Save me from curious conscience, that still lords
   Its strength for darkness, burrowing like a mole;
   Turn the key deftly in the oilèd wards,
   And seal the hushèd casket of my soul.

———— *o* ————

[J O H N   K E A T S]

From THE NIGHTINGALE

*N*o CLOUD, no relique of the sunken day
Distinguishes the West, no long thin slip
Of sullen light, no obscure trembling hues.
Come, we will rest on this old mossy bridge!
You see the glimmer of the stream beneath,
But hear no murmuring: it flows silently,
O'er its soft bed of verdure. All is still,
A balmy night! and though the stars be dim,
Yet let us think upon the vernal showers
That gladden the green earth, and we shall find
A pleasure in the dimness of the stars.
And hark! the Nightingale begins its song,
'Most musical, most melancholy' bird!
A melancholy bird? Oh! idle thought!
In Nature there is nothing melancholy.
But some night-wandering man whose heart was pierced
With the remembrance of a grievous wrong,
Or slow distemper, or neglected love,
(And so, poor wretch! filled all things with himself,
And made all gentle sounds tell back the tale
Of his own sorrow) he, and such as he,
First named these notes a melancholy strain.
And many a poet echoes the conceit;

POET WHO hath been building up the rhyme
When he had better far have stretched his limbs
Beside a brook in mossy forest-dell,
By sun or moon-light, to the influxes
Of shapes and sounds and shifting elements
Surrendering his whole spirit, of his song
And of his fame forgetful! so his fame
Should share in Nature's immortality,
A venerable thing! and so his song
Should make all Nature lovelier, and itself
Be loved like Nature! But 'twill not be so;
And youths and maidens most poetical,
Who lose the deepening twilights of the spring
In ball-rooms and hot theatres, they still
Full of meek sympathy must heave their sighs
O'er Philomela's pity-pleading strains.

MY FRIEND, and thou, our Sister! we have learnt
A different lore: we may not thus profane
Nature's sweet voices, always full of love
And joyance! 'Tis the merry Nightingale
That crowds, and hurries, and precipitates
With fast thick warble his delicious notes,
As he were fearful that an April night
Would be too short for him to utter forth
His love-chant, and disburthen his full soul
Of all its music!

———— o ————

[WILLIAM WORDSWORTH]

AN INCANTATION

WHEN THE MOON is on the wave,
  And the glow-worm in the grass,
  And the meteor on the grave,
  And the wisp on the morass;
  When the falling stars are shooting,
  And the answer'd owls are hooting,
  And the silent leaves are still
  In the shadow of the hill,
  Shall my soul be upon thine,
  With a power and with a sign.

THOUGH THY slumber may be deep,
  Yet thy spirit shall not sleep;
  There are shades which will not vanish,
  There are thoughts thou canst not banish;
  By a power to thee unknown,
  Thou canst never be alone;
  Thou art wrapt as with a shroud,
  Thou art gather'd in a cloud;
  And for ever shalt thou dwell
  In the spirit of this spell.

THOUGH THOU seest me not pass by,
  Thou shalt feel me with thine eye
  As a thing that, though unseen,
  Must be near thee, and hath been;
  And when in that secret dread
  Thou has turn'd around thy head,
  Thou shalt marvel I am not
  As thy shadow on the spot,

And the power which thou dost feel
Shall be what thou must conceal.

AND A magic voice and verse
Hath baptized thee with a curse;
And a spirit of the air
Hath begirt thee with a snare;
In the wind there is a voice
Shall forbid thee to rejoice;
And to thee shall night deny
All the quiet of her sky;
And the day shall have a sun,
Which shall make thee wish it done.

———— o ————

[GEORGE GORDON, LORD BYRON]

STANZAS FOR MUSIC

THERE BE NONE of Beauty's daughters
With a magic like thee;
And like music on the waters
Is thy sweet voice to me:
When, as if its sound were causing
The charmed ocean's pausing,
The waves lie still and gleaming,
And the lull'd winds seem dreaming:

AND THE midnight moon is weaving
Her bright chain o'er the deep;
Whose breast is gently heaving,
As an infant's asleep:
So the spirit bows before thee,
To listen and adore thee;
With a full but soft emotion,
Like the swell of Summer's ocean.

———— o ————

[GEORGE GORDON, LORD BYRON]

From THE PRELUDE, BOOK I

*I*N NOVEMBER days,
When vapours rolling down the valley made
A lonely scene more lonesome, among woods,
At noon and 'mid the calm of summer nights,
When, by the margin of the trembling lake,
Beneath the gloomy hills homeward I went
In solitude, such intercourse was mine;
Mine was it in the fields both day and night,
And by the waters, all the summer long.

AND IN the frosty season, when the sun
Was set, and visible for many a mile
The cottage windows blazed through twilight gloom,
I heeded not their summons: happy time
It was indeed for all of us—for me
It was a time of rapture!   Clear and loud
The village clock tolled six,—I wheeled about,
Proud and exulting like an untired horse
That cares not for his home.   All shod with steel,
We hissed along the polished ice in games
Confederate, imitative of the chase
And woodland pleasures,—the resounding horn,
The pack loud chiming, and the hunted hare.
So through the darkness and the cold we flew,
And not a voice was idle; with the din
Smitten, the precipices rang aloud;
The leafless trees and every ice crag
Tinkled like iron; while far distant hills
Into the tumult sent an alien sound

Of melancholy not unnoticed, while the stars
Eastward were sparkling clear, and in the west
The orange sky of evening died away.
Not seldom from the uproar I retired
Into a silent bay, or sportively
Glanced sideway, leaving the tumultuous throng,
To cut across the reflex of a star
That fled, and, flying still before me, gleamed
Upon the glassy plain; and oftentimes,
When we had given our bodies to the wind,
And all the shadowy banks on either side
Came sweeping through the darkness, spinning still
The rapid line of motion, then at once
Have I, reclining back upon my heels,
Stopped short; yet still the solitary cliffs
Wheeled by me—even as if the earth had rolled
With visible motion her diurnal round!
Behind me did they stretch in solemn train,
Feebler and feebler, and I stood and watched
Till all was tranquil as a dreamless sleep.

——— o ———

[W I L L I A M   W O R D S W O R T H]

The
CHANGING
SEASONS

THE SEASONS four, –
Green-kirtled Spring, flush
   Summer, golden store
In Autumn's sickle, Winter frosty
   hoar,
Join dance with shadowy Hours;

            ≈ KEATS

WORK WITHOUT HOPE

ALL NATURE seems at work. Slugs leave their lair—
The bees are stirring—birds are on the wing—
And Winter slumbering in the open air,
Wears on his smiling face a dream of Spring!
And I, the while, the sole unbusy thing,
Nor honey make, nor pair, nor build, nor sing.

YET WELL I ken the banks where amaranths blow,
Have traced the fount whence streams of nectar flow.
Bloom, O ye amaranths! bloom for whom ye may,
For me ye bloom not! Glide, rich streams, away!
With lips unbrightened, wreathless brow, I stroll:
And would you learn the spells that drowse my soul?
Work without Hope draws nectar in a sieve,
And Hope without an object cannot live.

—— o ——

[SAMUEL TAYLOR COLERIDGE]

From THE CLOUD

I BRING FRESH showers for the thirsting flowers,
From the seas and the streams;
I bear light shade for the leaves when laid
In their noon-day dreams.
From my wings are shaken the dews that waken
The sweet buds every one,
When rocked to rest on their mother's breast,
As she dances about the sun.
I wield the flail of the lashing hail,
And whiten the green plains under,
And then again I dissolve it in rain,
And laugh as I pass in thunder.

I SIFT THE snow on the mountains below,
And their great pines groan aghast;
And all the night 'tis my pillow white,
While I sleep in the arms of the blast.
Sublime on the towers of my skiey bowers,
Lightning my pilot sits,
In a cavern under is fettered the thunder,
It struggles and howls at fits;
Over earth and ocean, with gentle motion,
This pilot is guiding me,
Lured by the love of the genii that move
In the depths of the purple sea;
Over the rills, and the crags, and the hills,
Over the lakes and the plains,
Wherever he dream, under mountain or stream,
The Spirit he loves remains;

And I all the while bask in Heaven's blue smile,
Whilst he is dissolving in rains.

THE SANGUINE sunrise, with his meteor eyes,
And his burning plumes outspread,
Leaps on the back of my sailing rack,
When the morning star shines dead;
As on the jag of a mountain crag
Which an earthquake rocks and swings,
An eagle alit one moment may sit
In the light of its golden wings;
And when sunset may breathe, from the lit sea beneath,
Its ardours of rest and of love,
And the crimson pall of eve may fall
From the depths of Heaven above,
With wings folded I rest, on mine aëry nest,
As still as a brooding dove.

[PERCY BYSSHE SHELLEY]

From MARMION, CANTO III

*L*IKE APRIL morning clouds, that pass,
With varying shadow, o'er the grass,
And imitate, on field and furrow,
Life's chequer'd scene of joy and sorrow;
Like streamlet of the mountain north,
Now in a torrent racing forth,
Now winding slow its silver train,
And almost slumbering on the plain;
Like breezes of the autumn day,
Whose voice inconstant dies away,
And ever swells again as fast,
When the ear deems its murmur past;
Thus various, my romantic theme
Flits, winds, or sinks, a morning dream.
Yet pleas'd, our eye pursues the trace
Of Light and Shade's inconstant race;
Pleas'd, views the rivulet afar,
Weaving its maze irregular;
And pleas'd, we listen as the breeze
Heaves its wild sigh through autumn trees:
Then, wild as cloud, or stream, or gale,
Flow on, flow unconfin'd, my Tale!

———— o ————

[SIR WALTER SCOTT]

COMPOSED AT RYDAL
ON MAY MORNING, 1838

IF WITH OLD LOVE of you, dear Hills! I share
New love of many a rival image brought
From far, forgive the wanderings of my thought:
Nor art thou wronged, sweet May! when I compare
Thy present birth-morn with thy last, so fair,
So rich to me in favours. For my lot
Then was, within the famed Egerian Grot
To sit and muse, fanned by its dewy air
Mingling with thy soft breath! That morning too,
Warblers I heard their joy unbosoming
Amid the sunny, shadowy, Coloseum;
Heard them, unchecked by aught of saddening hue,
For victories there won by flower-crowned Spring,
Chant in full choir their innocent Te Deum.

———— o ————

[WILLIAM WORDSWORTH]

LINES WRITTEN IN EARLY SPRING

I HEARD a thousand blended notes,
While in a grove I sate reclined,
In that sweet mood when pleasant thoughts
Bring sad thoughts to the mind.

TO HER FAIR works did Nature link
The human soul that through me ran;
And much it grieved my heart to think
What man has made of man.

THROUGH primrose tufts, in that green bower,
The periwinkle trailed its wreaths;
And 'tis my faith that every flower
Enjoys the air it breathes.

THE BIRDS around me hopped and played,
Their thoughts I cannot measure:—
But the least motion which they made
It seemed a thrill of pleasure.

THE BUDDING twigs spread out their fan,
To catch the breezy air;
And I must think, do all I can,
That there was pleasure there.

IF THIS belief from heaven be sent,
If such be Nature's holy plan,
Have I not reason to lament
What man has made of man?

———— 0 ————

[WILLIAM WORDSWORTH]

'I WANDERED
LONELY AS A CLOUD'

I WANDERED lonely as a cloud
That floats on high o'er vales and hills,
When all at once I saw a crowd,
A host, of golden daffodils;
Beside the lake, beneath the trees,
Fluttering and dancing in the breeze.

CONTINUOUS as the stars that shine
And twinkle on the milky way,
They stretched in never-ending line
Along the margin of a bay:
Ten thousand saw I at a glance,
Tossing their heads in sprightly dance.

THE WAVES beside them danced; but they
Out-did the sparkling waves in glee:
A poet could not but be gay,
In such a jocund company:
I gazed—and gazed—but little thought
What wealth the show to me had brought:

FOR OFT, when on my couch I lie
In vacant or in pensive mood,
They flash upon that inward eye
Which is the bliss of solitude;
And then my heart with pleasure fills,
And dances with the daffodils.

———— *o* ————

[WILLIAM WORDSWORTH]

From LINES ON AN AUTUMNAL EVENING

O THOU WILD FANCY, check thy wing! No more
Those thin white flakes, those purple clouds explore!
Nor there with happy spirits speed thy flight
Bath'd in rich amber-glowing floods of light;
Nor in yon gleam, where slow descends the day,
With western peasants hail the morning ray!
Ah! rather bid the perish'd pleasures move,
A shadowy train, across the soul of Love!
O'er Disappointment's wintry desart fling
Each flower that wreath'd the dewy locks of SPRING,
When blushing, like a bride, from Hope's trim bower
She leapt, awaken'd by the pattering shower.

NOW SHEDS the sinking Sun a deeper gleam,
Aid, lovely Sorceress! aid thy Poet's dream!
With faery wand I bid the MAID arise,
Chaste Joyance dancing in her bright blue eyes;
As erst when from the Muses' calm abode
I came, with Learning's meed not unbestowed:
When, as she twin'd a laurel round my brow,
And met my kiss, and half return'd my vow,
O'er all my frame shot rapid my thrill'd heart,
And every nerve confess'd the electric dart.

O DEAR DECEIT! I see the Maiden rise,
Chaste Joyance dancing in her bright blue Eyes,
When first the lark high-soaring swells his throat,
Mocks the tir'd eye, and scatters the loud note,
I trace her footsteps on the accustom'd lawn,

I mark her glancing mid the gleams of dawn.
When the bent flower beneath the night-dew weeps
And on the lake the silver lustre sleeps,
Amid the paly radiance soft and sad
She meets my lonely path in moon-beams clad.
With her along the streamlet's brink I rove;
With her I list the warblings of the grove;
And seems in each low wind her voice to float
Lone-whispering Pity in each soothing note!

SPIRITS of LOVE! ye heard her name! Obey
The powerful spell, and to my haunt repair.
Whether on clust'ring pinions ye are there,
Where rich snows blossom on the Myrtle trees.
Or with fond languishment around my fair
Sigh in the loose luxuriance of her hair;
O heed the spell, and hither wing your way,
Like far-off music, voyaging the breeze!
SPIRITS! to you the infant Maid was given
Form'd by the wond'rous Alchemy of Heaven!
No fairer Maid does Love's wide empire know,
No fairer Maid e'er heav'd the bosom's snow.
A thousand Loves around her forehead fly;
A thousand Loves sit melting in her eye;
Love lights her smile—in Joy's red nectar dips
The flamy rose, and plants it on her lips!

——— *0* ———

[SAMUEL TAYLOR COLERIDGE]

From ODE TO THE WEST WIND

O WILD WEST WIND, thou breath of Autumn's being,
Thou, from whose unseen presence the leaves dead
Are driven, like ghosts from an enchanter fleeing,

YELLOW, and black, and pale, and hectic red,
Pestilence-stricken multitudes: O thou,
Who chariotest to their dark wintry bed

THE WINGÈD seeds, where they lie cold and low,
Each like a corpse within its grave, until
Thine azure sister of the Spring shall blow

HER CLARION o'er the dreaming earth, and fill
(Driving sweet buds like flocks to feed in air)
With living hues and odours plain and hill:

WILD SPIRIT, which art moving everywhere;
Destroyer and Preserver; hear, O hear!

———— *0* ————

[PERCY BYSSHE SHELLEY]

TO AUTUMN

SEASON OF MISTS and mellow fruitfulness!
  Close bosom-friend of the maturing sun;
  Conspiring with him how to load and bless
  With fruit the vines that round the thatch-eaves run;
  To bend with apples the moss'd cottage-trees,
  And fill all fruit with ripeness to the core;
  To swell the gourd, and plump the hazel shells
  With a sweet kernel; to set budding more,
  And still more, later flowers for the bees,
  Until they think warm days will never cease,
  For Summer has o'er-brimm'd their clammy cells.

WHO HATH not seen thee oft amid thy store?
  Sometimes whoever seeks abroad may find
  Thee sitting careless on a granary floor,
  Thy hair soft-lifted by the winnowing wind;
  Or on a half-reap'd furrow sound asleep,
  Drowsed with the fumes of poppies, while thy hook
  Spares the next swath and all its twinèd flowers;
  And sometimes like a gleaner thou dost keep
  Steady thy laden head across a brook;
  Or by a cider-press, with patient look,
  Thou watchest the last oozings, hours by hours.

WHERE ARE the songs of Spring?   Ay, where are they?

Think not of them, thou hast thy music too,

While barrèd clouds bloom the soft-dying day,

And touch the stubble-plains with rosy hue;

Then in a wailful choir the small gnats mourn

Among the river sallows, borne aloft

Or sinking as the light wind lives or dies;

And full-grown lambs loud bleat from hilly bourn;

Hedge-crickets sing; and now with treble soft

The redbreast whistles from a garden-croft,

And gathering swallows twitter in the skies.

———— 0 ————

[JOHN KEATS]

NOVEMBER

*T*HE MELLOW YEAR is hasting to its close;
    The little birds have almost sung their last,
    Their small notes twitter in the dreary blast—
    That shrill-piped harbinger of early snows;
    The patient beauty of the scentless rose,
    Oft with the Morn's hoar crystal quaintly glass'd,
    Hangs, a pale mourner for the summer past,
    And makes a little summer where it grows:
    In the chill sunbeam of the faint brief day
    The dusky waters shudder as they shine,
    The russet leaves obstruct the struggling way
    Of oozy brooks, which no deep banks define,
    And the gaunt woods, in ragged, scant array,
    Wrap their old limbs with sombre ivy twine.

----- *o* -----

[HARTLEY COLERIDGE]

MUTABILITY

*F*ROM LOW to high doth dissolution climb,
　And sink from high to low, along a scale
　Of awful notes, whose concord shall not fail;
　A musical but melancholy chime,
　Which they can hear who meddle not with crime,
　Nor avarice, nor over-anxious care.
　Truth fails not; but her outward forms that bear
　The longest date do melt like frosty rime,
　That in the morning whitened hill and plain
　And is no more; drop like the tower sublime
　Of yesterday, which royally did wear
　His crown of weeds, but could not even sustain
　Some casual shout that broke the silent air,
　Or the unimaginable touch of Time.

———— *o* ————

[WILLIAM WORDSWORTH]

THE QUESTION

I DREAMED that, as I wandered by the way,
Bare Winter suddenly was changed to Spring,
And gentle odours led my steps astray,
Mixed with a sound of waters murmuring
Along a shelving bank of turf, which lay
Under a copse, and hardly dared to fling
Its green arms round the bosom of the stream,
But kissed it and then fled, as thou mightest in dream.

THERE GREW pied wind-flowers and violets,
Daisies, those pearled Arcturi of the earth,
The constellated flower that never sets;
Faint oxslips; tender bluebells, at whose birth
The sod scarce heaved; and that tall flower that wets—
Like a child, half in tenderness and mirth—
Its mother's face with Heaven's collected tears,
When the low wind, its playmate's voice, it hears.

AND IN the warm hedge grew lush eglantine,
Green cowbind and the moonlight-coloured may,
And cherry-blossoms, and white cups, whose wine
Was the bright dew, yet drained not by the day;
And wild roses, and ivy serpentine,
With its dark buds and leaves, wandering astray;
And flowers azure, black, and streaked with gold,
Fairer than any wakened eyes behold.

AND NEARER to the river's trembling edge
There grew broad flag-flowers, purple pranked with white,
And starry river buds among the sedge,
And floating water-lilies, broad and bright,
Which lit the oak that overhung the hedge
With moonlight beams of their own watery light;
And bulrushes, and reeds of such deep green
As soothed the dazzled eye with sober sheen.

METHOUGHT that of these visionary flowers
I made a nosegay, bound in such a way
That the same hues, which in their natural bowers
Were mingled or opposed, the like array
Kept these imprisoned children of the Hours
Within my hand,—and then, elate and gay,
I hastened to the spot whence I had come,
That I might there present it!—Oh! to whom?

———— 0 ————

[PERCY BYSSHE SHELLEY]

The
AGES

=== O F ===

MAN

THE CHILD is father of the Man;
And I could wish my days to be
Bound each to each by natural piety.

≈ WORDSWORTH

THE HUMAN SEASONS

*F*OUR SEASONS fill the measure of the year;
 There are four seasons in the mind of man:
 He has his lusty Spring, when fancy clear
 Takes in all beauty with an easy span:
 He has his Summer, when luxuriously
 Spring's honey'd cud of youthful thought he loves
 To ruminate, and by such dreaming high
 Is nearest unto Heaven: quiet coves
 His soul has in its Autumn, when his wings
 He furleth close; contented so to look
 On mists in idleness—to let fair things
 Pass by unheeded as a threshold brook.
 He has his Winter too of pale misfeature,
 Or else he would forego his mortal nature.

———— *o* ————

[JOHN KEATS]

From THE PRELUDE, BOOK I

INTRODUCTION — CHILDHOOD AND SCHOOL-TIME

*F*AIR SEED-TIME had my soul, and I grew up
   Fostered alike by beauty and by fear:
   Much favoured in my birth-place, and no less
   In that belovèd Vale to which erelong
   We were transplanted—there were we let loose
   For sports of wider range.   Ere I had told
   Ten birth-days, when among the mountain slopes
   Frost, and the breath of frosty wind, had snapped
   The last autumnal crocus, 'twas my joy
   With store of springes o'er my shoulder hung
   To range the open heights where woodcocks run
   Along the smooth green turf.   Through half the night,
   Scudding away from snare to snare, I plied
   That anxious visitation;—moon and stars
   Were shining o'er my head.   I was alone,
   And seemed to be a trouble to the peace
   That dwelt among them.   Sometimes it befell
   In these night wanderings, that a strong desire
   O'erpowered my better reason, and the bird
   Which was the captive of another's toil
   Became my prey; and when the deed was done
   I heard among the solitary hills
   Low breathing coming after me, and sounds
   Of undistinguishable motion, steps
   Almost as silent as the turf they trod.

   NOR LESS, when spring had warmed the cultured Vale,
   Roved we as plunderers where the mother-bird
   Had in high places built her lodge; though mean

Our object and inglorious, yet the end
Was not ignoble.   Oh! when I have hung
Above the raven's nest, by knots of grass
And half-inch fissures in the slippery rock
But ill sustained, and almost (so it seemed)
Suspended by the blast that blew amain,
Shouldering the naked crag, oh, at that time
While on the perilous ridge I hung alone,
With what strange utterance did the loud dry wind
Blow through my ear! the sky seemed not a sky
Of earth—and with what motion moved the clouds!

DUST AS we are, the immortal spirit grows
Like harmony in music; there is a dark
Inscrutable workmanship that reconciles
Discordant elements, makes them cling together
In one society.   How strange, that all
The terrors, pains, and early miseries,
Regrets, vexations, lassitudes interfused
Within my mind, should e'er have borne a part,
And that a needful part, in making up
The calm existence that is mine when I
Am worthy of myself!   Praise to the end!
Thanks to the means which Nature deigned to employ;
Whether her fearless vistings, or those
That came with soft alarm, like hurtless light
Opening the peaceful clouds; or she may use
Severer interventions, ministry
More palpable, as best might suit her aim.

——— *o* ———

[W I L L I A M   W O R D S W O R T H]

'LONG TIME A CHILD'

LONG TIME a child, and still a child, when years
　　Had painted manhood on my cheek, was I;
　　For yet I lived like one not born to die;
　　A thriftless prodigal of smiles and tears,
　　No hope I needed, and I knew no fears.
　　But sleep, though sweet, is only sleep, and waking,
　　I waked to sleep no more, at once o'ertaking
　　The vanguard of my age, with all arrears
　　Of duty on my back. Nor child, nor man,
　　Nor youth, nor sage, I find my head is grey,
　　For I have lost the race I never ran:
　　A rathe December blights my lagging May;
　　And still I am a child, tho' I be old,
　　Time is my debtor for my years untold.

——— o ———

[HARTLEY COLERIDGE]

THERE WAS A BOY

*T*HERE WAS a Boy: ye knew him well, ye cliffs
And islands of Winander!—many a time
At evening, when the earliest stars began
To move along the edges of the hills,
Rising or setting, would he stand alone
Beneath the trees or by the glimmering lake,
And there, with fingers interwoven, both hands
Pressed closely palm to palm, and to his mouth
Uplifted, he, as through an instrument,
Blew mimic hootings to the silent owls,
That they might answer him; and they would shout
Across the watery vale, and shout again,
Responsive to his call, with quivering peals,
And long halloos and screams, and echoes loud,
Redoubled and redoubled, concourse wild
Of jocund din; and, when a lengthened pause
Of silence came and baffled his best skill,
Then sometimes, in that silence while he hung
Listening, a gentle shock of mild surprise
Has carried far into his heart the voice
Of mountain torrents; or the visible scene
Would enter unawares into his mind,
With all its solemn imagery, its rocks,
Its woods, and that uncertain heaven, received
Into the bosom of the steady lake.

THIS BOY was taken from his mates, and died

In childhood, ere he was full twelve years old.

Fair is the spot, most beautiful the vale

Where he was born; the grassy churchyard hangs

Upon a slope above the village school,

And through that churchyard when my way had led

On summer evenings, I believe that there

A long half hour together I have stood

Mute, looking at the grave in which he lies!

———— o ————

[WILLIAM WORDSWORTH]

'THREE YEARS SHE GREW
IN SUN AND SHOWER'

THREE YEARS she grew in sun and shower,
Then Nature said, 'A lovelier flower
On earth was never sown;
This Child I to myself will take;
She shall be mine, and I will make
A Lady of my own.

'MYSELF WILL to my darling be
Both law and impulse: and with me
The Girl, in rock and plain,
In earth and heaven, in glade and bower,
Shall feel an overseeing power
To kindle or restrain.

'SHE SHALL be sportive as the fawn
That wild with glee across the lawn,
Or up the mountain springs;
And hers shall be the breathing balm,
And hers the silence and the calm
Of mute insensate things.

'THE FLOATING clouds their state shall lend
To her; for her the willow bend;
Nor shall she fail to see
Even in the motions of the Storm
Grace that shall mould the Maiden's form
By silent sympathy.

'THE STARS of midnight shall be dear
To her; and she shall lean her ear
In many a secret place
Where rivulets dance their wayward round,
And beauty born of murmuring sound
Shall pass into her face.

'AND VITAL feelings of delight
Shall rear her form to stately height,
Her virgin bosom swell;
Such thoughts to Lucy I will give
While she and I together live
Here in this happy dell.'

THUS NATURE spake— The work was done—
How soon my Lucy's race was run!
She died, and left to me
This heath, this calm, and quiet scene;
The memory of what has been,
And never more will be.

———— 0 ————

[WILLIAM WORDSWORTH]

From FROST AT MIDNIGHT

*B*UT o! how oft,
How oft, at school, with most believing mind,
Presageful, have I gazed upon the bars,
To watch that fluttering *stranger*! and as oft
With unclosed lids, already had I dreamt
Of my sweet birth-place, and the old church-tower,
Whose bells, the poor man's only music, rang
From morn to evening, all the hot Fair-day,
So sweetly, that they stirred and haunted me
With a wild pleasure, falling on mine ear
Most like articulate sounds of things to come!
So gazed I, till the soothing things, I dreamt,
Lulled me to sleep, and sleep prolonged my dreams!
And so I brooded all the following morn,
Awed by the stern preceptor's face, mine eye
Fixed with mock study on my swimming book:
Save if the door half opened, and I snatched
A hasty glance, and still my heart leaped up,
For still I hoped to see the *stranger's* face,
Townsman, or aunt, or sister more beloved,
My play-mate when we both were clothed alike!

DEAR BABE, that sleepest cradled by my side,
Whose gentle breathings, heard in this deep calm,
Fill up the interspersèd vacancies
And momentary pauses of the thought!
My babe so beautiful! it thrills my heart
With tender gladness, thus to look at thee,
And think that thou shalt learn far other lore,
And in far other scenes! For I was reared

In the great city, pent 'mid cloisters dim,
And saw nought lovely but the sky and stars.
But *thou*, my babe! shalt wander like a breeze
By lakes and sandy shores, beneath the crags
Of ancient mountain, and beneath the clouds,
Which image in their bulk both lakes and shores
And mountain crags: so shalt thou see and hear
The lovely shapes and sounds intelligible
Of that eternal language, which thy God
Utters, who from eternity doth teach
Himself in all, and all things in himself.
Great universal Teacher! he shall mould
Thy spirit, and by giving make it ask.

THEREFORE all seasons shall be sweet to thee,
Whether the summer clothe the general earth
With greenness, or the redbreast sit and sing
Betwixt the tufts of snow on the bare branch
Of mossy apple-tree, while the nigh thatch
Smokes in the sun-thaw; whether the eave-drops fall
Heard only in the trances of the blast,
Or if the secret ministry of frost
Shall hang them up in silent icicles,
Quietly shining to the quiet Moon.

——— *0* ———

[S A M U E L   T A Y L O R   C O L E R I D G E]

CHARACTERISTICS OF A CHILD
THREE YEARS OLD

*L*OVING SHE IS, and tractable, though wild;
　　And Innocence hath privilege in her
　　To dignify arch looks and laughing eyes
　　And feats of cunning; and the pretty round
　　Of trespasses, affected to provoke
　　Mock-chastisement and partnership in play.
　　And, as a faggot sparkles on the hearth,
　　Not less if unattended and alone
　　Than when both young and old sit gathered round
　　And take delight in its activity;
　　Even so this happy Creature of herself
　　Is all-sufficient; solitude to her
　　Is blithe society, who fills the air
　　With gladness and involuntary songs.
　　Light are her sallies as the tripping fawn's
　　Forth-startled from the fern where she lay couched;
　　Unthought-of, unexpected, as the stir
　　Of the soft breeze ruffling the meadow-flowers,
　　Or from before it chasing wantonly
　　The many-coloured images imprest
　　Upon the bosom of a placid lake.

———— *o* ————

[WILLIAM WORDSWORTH]

YOUTH AND AGE

*V*ERSE, A BREEZE mid blossoms straying,
  Where Hope clung feeding, like a bee—
Both were mine! Life went a maying
With Nature, Hope, and Poesy,
  When I was young!

WHEN I was young?—Ah, woful When!
Ah! for the change 'twixt Now and Then!
This breaking house not built with hands,
This body that does me grievous wrong,
O'er aery cliffs and glittering sands,
How lightly then it flashed along:—
Like those trim skiffs, unknown of yore,
On winding lakes and rivers wide,
That ask no aid of sail or oar,
That fear no spite of wind or tide!
Nought cared this body for wind or weather
When Youth and I lived in't together.

FLOWERS are lovely; Love is flower-like;
Friendship is a sheltering tree;
O! the joys, that came down shower-like,
Of Friendship, Love, and Liberty,
  Ere I was old!
Ere I was old? Ah woful Ere,
Which tells me, Youth's no longer here!
O Youth! for years so many and sweet,
'Tis known, that Thou and I were one,
I'll think it but a fond conceit—
It cannot be that Thou art gone!

THY VESPER-bell hath not yet toll'd:
And thou wert aye a masker bold!
What strange disguise hast now put on,
To make believe, that thou art gone?
I see these locks in silvery slips,
This drooping gait, this altered size:
But Spring-tide blossoms on thy lips,
And tears take sunshine from thine eyes!
Life is but thought: so think I will
That Youth and I are house-mates still.

DEW-DROPS are the gems of morning,
But the tears of mournful eve!
Where no hope is, life's a warning
That only serves to make us grieve,
When we are old:

THAT ONLY serves to make us grieve
With oft and tedious taking-leave,
Like some poor nigh-related guest,
That may not rudely be dismist;
Yet hath outstay'd his welcome while,
And tells the jest without the smile.

——— 0 ———

[SAMUEL TAYLOR COLERIDGE]

From THE EXCURSION

Such was the Boy—but for the growing Youth
What soul was his, when, from the naked top
Of some bold headland, he beheld the sun
Rise up, and bathe the world in light! He looked—
Ocean and earth, the solid frame of earth
And ocean's liquid mass, beneath him lay
In gladness and deep joy. The clouds were touched,
And in their silent faces could he read
Unutterable love. Sound needed none,
Nor any voice of joy; his spirit drank
The spectacle: sensation, soul, and form
All melted into him; they swallowed up
His animal being; in them did he live,
And by them did he live; they were his life.
In such access of mind, in such high hour
Of visitation from the living God,
Thought was not; in enjoyment it expired.
No thanks he breathed, he proffered no request;
Rapt into still communion that transcends
The imperfect offices of prayer and praise,
His mind was a thanksgiving to the power
That made him; it was blessedness and love!

———— o ————

[WILLIAM WORDSWORTH]

THE FLOWER THAT SMILES TODAY

THE FLOWER that smiles today
Tomorrow dies;
All that we wish to stay
Tempts and then flies;
What is this world's delight?
Lightning, that mocks the night,
Brief even as bright.—

VIRTUE, how frail it is!—
Friendship, how rare!—
Love, how it sells poor bliss
For proud despair!
But these, though soon they fall,
Survive their joy, and all
Which ours we call.—

WHILST SKIES are blue and bright,
Whilst flowers are gay,
Whilst eyes that change ere night
Make glad the day;
Whilst yet the calm hours creep,
Dream thou—and from thy sleep
Then wake to weep.

———— o ————

[PERCY BYSSHE SHELLEY]

From TO A YOUNG FRIEND, ON HIS PROPOSING TO DOMESTICATE WITH THE AUTHOR

*A*M O U N T, not wearisome and bare and steep,
But a green mountain variously up-piled,
Where o'er the jutting rocks soft mosses creep,
Or colour'd lichens with slow oozing weep;
Where cypress and the darker yew start wild;
And, 'mid the summer torrent's gentle dash
Dance brighten'd the red clusters of the ash;
Beneath whose boughs, by those still sounds beguil'd,
Calm Pensiveness might muse herself to sleep;
Till haply startled by some fleecy dam,
That rustling on the bushy cliff above
With melancholy bleat of anxious love,
Made meek enquiry for her wandering lamb:
Such a green mountain 'twere most sweet to climb,
E'en while the bosom ach'd with loneliness—
How more than sweet, if some dear friend should bless
The adventurous toil, and up the path sublime
Now lead, now follow: the glad landscape round,
Wide and more wide, increasing without bound!

O THEN 'twere loveliest sympathy, to mark
The berries of the half-uprooted ash
Dripping and bright; and list the torrent's dash,—
Beneath the cypress, or the yew more dark,
Seated at ease, on some smooth mossy rock;
In social silence now, and now to unlock
The treasur'd heart; arm linked in friendly arm,

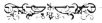

Save if the one, his muse's witching charm
Muttering brow-bent, at unwatch'd distance lag;
Till high o'er head his beckoning friend appears,
And from the forehead of the topmost crag
Shouts eagerly: for haply *there* uprears
That shadowing Pine its old romantic limbs,
Which latest shall detain the enamour'd sight
Seen from below, when eve the valley dims,
Tinged yellow with the rich departing light;
And haply, bason'd in some unsunn'd cleft,
A beauteous spring, the rock's collected tears,
Sleeps shelter'd there, scarce wrinkled by the gale!
Together thus, the world's vain turmoil left,
Stretch'd on the crag, and shadow'd by the pine,
And bending o'er the clear delicious fount,
Ah! dearest youth! it were a lot divine
To cheat our noons in moralizing mood,
While west-winds fann'd our temples toil-bedew'd:
Then downwards slope, oft pausing, from the mount,
To some lone mansion, in some woody dale,
Where smiling with blue eye, Domestic Bliss
Gives *this* the Husband's, *that* the Brother's kiss!

———— *o* ————

[S A M U E L T A Y L O R C O L E R I D G E]

ODE TO TRANQUILLITY

*T*RANQUILLITY! thou better name
Than all the family of Fame!
Thou ne'er wilt my riper age
To low intrigue, or factious rage;
For oh! dear child of thoughtful Truth,
To thee I gave my early youth,
And left the bark, and blest the steadfast shore,
Ere yet the tempest rose and scared me with its roar.

WHO LATE and lingering seeks thy shrine,
On him but seldom, Power divine,
Thy spirit rests! Satiety
And Sloth, poor counterfeits of thee,
Mock the tired worldling. Idle Hope
And dire Remembrance interlope,
To vex the feverish slumber of the mind:
The bubble floats before, the spectre stalks behind.

BUT ME thy gentle hand will lead
At morning through the accustomed mead;
And in the sultry summer's heat
Will build me up a mossy seat;
And when the gust of Autumn crowds,
And breaks the busy moonlight clouds,
Thou best the thought canst raise, the heart attune,
Light as the busy clouds, calm as the gliding moon.

THE FEELING heart, the searching soul,
To thee I dedicate the whole!
And while within myself I trace
The greatness of some future race,
Aloof with hermit-eye I scan
The present works of present man—
A wild and dream-like trade of blood and guile,
Too foolish for a tear, too wicked for a smile!

———— o ————

[SAMUEL TAYLOR COLERIDGE]

LIFE
DEATH
AND
ETERNITY

MUSIC, when soft voices die,
Vibrates in the memory, –
Odours, when sweet violets sicken,
Live within the sense they quicken –

≈ SHELLEY

From ENDYMION, BOOK I

A THING OF beauty is a joy for ever:
　　Its loveliness increases; it will never
　　Pass into nothingness; but still will keep
　　A bower quiet for us, and a sleep
　　Full of sweet dreams, and health, and quiet breathing.
　　Therefore, on every morrow, are we wreathing
　　A flowery band to bind us to the earth,
　　Spite of despondence, of the inhuman dearth
　　Of noble natures, of the gloomy days,
　　Of all the unhealthy and o'er-darken'd ways
　　Made for our searching: yes. in spite of all,
　　Some shape of beauty moves away the pall
　　From our dark spirits.　　Such the sun, the moon,
　　Trees old and young, sprouting a shady boon
　　For simple sheep; and such are daffodils
　　With the green world they live in; and clear rills
　　That for themselves a cooling covert make
　　'Gainst the hot season; the mid-forest brake,
　　Rich with a sprinkling of fair musk-rose blooms:
　　And such too is the grandeur of the dooms
　　We have imagined for the mighty dead;
　　All lovely tales that we have heard or read:
　　An endless fountain of immortal drink,
　　Pouring unto us from the heaven's brink.

———— *o* ————

[JOHN KEATS]

From THIS LIME-TREE BOWER
MY PRISON

WELL, THEY are gone, and here must I remain,
This lime-tree bower my prison! I have lost
Beauties and feelings, such as would have been
Most sweet to my remembrance even when age
Had dimm'd mine eyes to blindness! They, meanwhile,
Friends, whom I never more may meet again,
On springy heath, along the hill-top edge,
Wander in gladness, and wind down, perchance,
To that still roaring dell, of which I told;
The roaring dell, o'erwooded, narrow, deep,
And only speckled by the mid-day sun;
Where its slim trunk the ash from rock to rock
Flings arching like a bridge;—that branchless ash,
Unsunn'd and damp, whose few poor yellow leaves
Ne'er tremble in the gale, yet tremble still,
Fann'd by the water-fall! and there my friends
Behold the dark green file of long lank weeds,
That all at once (a most fantastic sight!)
Still nod and drip beneath the dripping edge
Of the blue clay-stone.

NOW MY friends emerge
Beneath the wide wide Heaven—and view again
The many-steepled tract magnificent
Of hilly fields and meadows, and the sea,
With some fair bark, perhaps, whose sails light up
The slip of smooth clear blue betwixt two Isles
Of purple shadow! Yes! they wander on
In gladness all; but thou, methinks, most glad,

My gentle-hearted Charles! for thou hast pined
And hunger'd after Nature, many a year,
In the great City pent, winning thy way
With sad yet patient soul, through evil and pain
And strange calamity! Ah! slowly sink
Behind the western ridge, thou glorious Sun!
Shine in the slant beams of the sinking orb,
Ye purple heath-flowers! richlier burn, ye clouds!
Live in the yellow light, ye distant groves!
And kindle, thou blue Ocean! So my friend
Struck with deep joy may stand, as I have stood,
Silent with swimming sense; yea, gazing round
On the wide landscape, gaze till all doth seem
Less gross than bodily; and of such hues
As veil the Almighty Spirit, when yet he makes
Spirits perceive his presence.

———— 0 ————

[SAMUEL TAYLOR COLERIDGE]

'WHEN I HAVE FEARS'

WHEN I have fears that I may cease to be
　　　Before my pen has glean'd my teeming brain,
　　　Before high-piled books, in charact'ry,
　　　Hold like rich garners the full-ripen'd grain;
　　　When I behold, upon the night's starr'd face,
　　　Huge cloudy symbols of a high romance,
　　　And feel that I may never live to trace
　　　Their shadows, with the magic hand of chance;
　　　And when I feel, fair creature of an hour!
　　　That I shall never look upon thee more,
　　　Never have relish in the faery power
　　　Of unreflecting love!—then on the shore
　　　Of the wide world I stand alone, and think,
　　　Till Love and Fame to nothingness do sink.

———— o ————

[JOHN KEATS]

SONG

*R*ARELY, RARELY, comest thou,
  Spirit of Delight!
Wherefore hast thou left me now
  Many a day and night?
Many a weary night and day
'Tis since thou art fled away.

HOW SHALL ever one like me
  Win thee back again?
With the joyous and the free
  Thou wilt scoff at pain.
Spirit false! that hast forgot
All but those who need thee not.

AS A LIZARD with the shade
  Of a trembling leaf,
Thou with sorrow art dismayed;
  Even the sighs of grief
Reproach thee, that thou art not near,
And reproach thou wilt not hear.

LET ME set my mournful ditty
  To a merry measure;
Thou wilt never come for pity,
  Thou wilt come for pleasure;
Pity then will cut away
Those cruel wings, and thou wilt stay.

I LOVE all that thou lovest,
Spirit of Delight!
The fresh Earth in new leaves dressed,
And the starry night;
Autumn evening, and the morn
When the golden mists are born.

I LOVE snow, and all the forms
Of the radiant frost;
I love waves and winds and storms—
Every thing almost
Which is Nature's, and may be
Untainted by man's misery.

I LOVE tranquil solitude,
And such society
As is quiet, wise and good;
Between thee and me
What difference?—but thou dost possess
The things I seek, not love them less.

I LOVE Love—though he has wings,
And like light can flee—
But above all other things,
Spirit, I love thee—
Thou art Love and Life! O come,
Make once more my heart thy home.

———— o ————

[PERCY BYSSHE SHELLEY]

'MY DAYS AMONG THE DEAD
ARE PAST'

MY DAYS among the Dead are past;
  Around me I behold,
Where'er these casual eyes are cast,
  The mighty minds of old;
My never-failing friends are they,
With whom I converse day by day.

WITH THEM I take delight in weal,
  And seek relief in woe;
And while I understand and feel
  How much to them I owe,
My cheeks have often been bedew'd
With tears of thoughtful gratitude.

MY THOUGHTS are with the Dead, with them
  I live in long-past years,
Their virtues love, their faults condemn,
  Partake their hopes and fears,
And from their lessons seek and find
Instruction with an humble mind.

MY HOPES are with the Dead, anon
  My place with them will be,
And I with them shall travel on
  Through all Futurity;
Yet leaving here a name, I trust,
That will not perish in the dust.

——— 0 ———

[ROBERT SOUTHEY]

LINES

*L*OUD IS the Vale! the Voice is up
    With which she speaks when storms are gone,
    A mighty unison of streams!
    Of all her Voices, One!

    LOUD IS the Vale;—this inland Depth
    In peace is roaring like the Sea;
    Yon star upon the mountain-top
    Is listening quietly.

    SAD WAS I, even to pain deprest,
    Importunate and heavy load!
    The Comforter hath found me here,
    Upon this lonely road;

    AND MANY thousands now are sad—
    Wait the fulfilment of their fear;
    For he must die who is their stay,
    Their glory disappear.

    A POWER is passing from the earth
    To breathless Nature's dark abyss;
    But when the great and good depart
    What is it more than this—

    THAT MAN, who is from God sent forth,
    Doth yet again to God return?—
    Such ebb and flow must ever be,
    Then wherefore should we mourn?

———— *0* ————

[WILLIAM WORDSWORTH]

From REFLECTIONS ON HAVING LEFT A PLACE OF RETIREMENT

*O*FT WITH patient ear
Long-listening to the viewless sky-lark's note
(Viewless, or haply for a moment seen
Gleaming on sunny wings) in whisper'd tones
I've said to my Belovéd, 'Such, sweet Girl!
The inobtrusive song of Happiness,
Unearthly minstrelsy! then only heard
When the Soul seeks to hear; when all is hush'd,
And the Heart listens!'

BUT THE time, when first
From that low Dell, steep up the stony Mount
I climb'd with perilous toil and reach'd the top,
Oh! what a goodly scene! *Here* the bleak mount,
The bare bleak mountain speckled thin with sheep;
Grey clouds, that shadowing spot the sunny fields;
And river, now with bushy rocks o'er-brow'd,
Now winding bright and full, with naked banks;
And seats, and lawns, the Abbey and the wood,
And cots, and hamlets, and faint city-spire;
The Channel *there*, the Islands and white sails,
Dim coasts, and cloud-like hills, and shoreless Ocean—
It seem'd like Omnipresence! God, methought,
Had built him there a Temple: the whole World
Seem'd *imag'd* in its vast circumference:
No *wish* profan'd my overwhelméd heart.
Blest hour! It was a luxury,—to be!

AH! QUIET Dell! dear Cot, and Mount sublime!
I was constrain'd to quit you. Was it right,
While my unnumber'd brethren toil'd and bled,
That I should dream away the entrusted hours
On rose-leaf beds, pampering the coward heart
With feelings all too delicate for use?
Sweet is the tear that from some Howard's eye
Drops on the cheek of one he lifts from earth:
And he that works me good with unmov'd face,
Does it but half: he chills me while he aids,
My benefactor, not my brother man!
Yet even this, this cold beneficence
Praise, praise it, O my Soul! oft as thou scann'st
The sluggard Pity's vision-weaving tribe!
Who sigh for Wretchedness, yet shun the Wretched,
Nursing in some delicious solitude
Their slothful loves and dainty sympathies!
I therefore go, and join head, heart, and hand,
Active and firm, to fight the bloodless fight
Of Science, Freedom, and the Truth in Christ.

YET OFT when after honourable toil
Rests the tir'd mind, and waking loves to dream,
My spirit shall revisit thee, dear Cot!
Thy Jasmin and thy window-peeping Rose,
And Myrtles fearless of the mild sea-air.
And I shall sigh fond wishes—sweet Abode!
Ah!—had none greater! And that all had such!
It might be so—but the time is not yet.
Speed it, O Father! Let thy Kingdom come!

[SAMUEL TAYLOR COLERIDGE]

SONG

A SPIRIT haunts the year's last hours
    Dwelling amid these yellowing bowers:
    To himself he talks;
    For at eventide, listening earnestly,
    At his work you may hear him sob and sigh
    In the walks;
    Earthward he boweth the heavy stalks
    Of the mouldering flowers:
    Heavily hangs the broad sunflower
    Over its grave i' the earth so chilly;
    Heavily hangs the hollyhock,
    Heavily hangs the tiger-lily.

    THE AIR is damp, and hush'd, and close,
    As a sick man's room when he taketh repose
    An hour before death;
    My very heart faints and my whole soul grieves
    At the moist rich smell of the rotting leaves,
    And the breath
    Of the fading edges of box beneath,
    And the year's last rose.
    Heavily hangs the broad sunflower
    Over its grave i' the earth so chilly;
    Heavily hangs the hollyhock,
    Heavily hangs the tiger-lily.

———— *o* ————

[ALFRED, LORD TENNYSON]

LA BELLE DAME SANS MERCI

O W H A T can ail thee, knight-at-arms,
  Alone and palely loitering?
  The sedge is wither'd from the lake,
  And no birds sing.

O WHAT can ail thee, knight-at-arms,
  So haggard and so woe-begone?
  The squirrel's granary is full,
  And the harvest's done.

I SEE a lily on thy brow
  With anguish moist and fever dew,
  And on thy cheeks a fading rose
  Fast withereth too.

I MET a lady in the meads,
  Full beautiful—a faery's child,
  Her hair was long, her foot was light,
  And her eyes were wild.

I MADE a garland for her head,
  And bracelets too, and fragrant zone,
  She look'd at me as she did love,
  And made sweet moan.

I SET her on my pacing steed,
  And nothing else saw all day long,
  For sidelong would she bend, and sing
  A faery's song.

SHE FOUND me roots of relish sweet,
And honey wild, and manna dew,
And sure in language strange she said—
'I love thee true!'

SHE TOOK me to her elfin grot,
And there she wept and sigh'd full sore,
And there I shut her wild, wild eyes
With kisses four.

AND THERE she lullèd me asleep,
And there I dream'd –ah! woe betide!
The latest dream I ever dream'd
On the cold hill's side.

I SAW pale kings and princes too,
Pale warriors, death-pale were they all;
They cried—'La Belle Dame sans Merci
Hath thee in thrall!'

I SAW their starved lips in the gloam,
With horrid warning gapèd wide,
And I awoke and found me here,
On the cold hill's side.

AND THIS is why I sojourn here,
Alone and palely loitering,
Though the sedge is wither'd from the lake,
And no birds sing.

———— 0 ————

[JOHN KEATS]

'A SLUMBER DID MY SPIRIT SEAL'

A SLUMBER did my spirit seal;
I had no human fears:
She seemed a thing that could not feel
The touch of earthly years.

NO MOTION has she now, no force;
She neither hears nor sees;
Rolled round in earth's diurnal course,
With rocks, and stones, and trees.

—— *o* ——

[WILLIAM WORDSWORTH]

From HYMN TO
INTELLECTUAL BEAUTY

*T*HE AWFUL shadow of some unseen Power
    Floats though unseen amongst us,—visiting
    This various world with as inconstant wing
    As summer winds that creep from flower to flower.—
    Like moonbeams that behind some piny mountain shower,
    It visits with inconstant glance
    Each human heart and countenance;
    Like hues and harmonies of evening,—
    Like clouds in starlight widely spread,—
    Like memory of music fled,—
    Like aught that for its grace may be
    Dear, and yet dearer for its mystery.

    SPIRIT OF BEAUTY, that doth consecrate
    With thine own hues all thou dost shine upon
    Of human thought or form,—where art thou gone?
    Why dost thou pass away and leave our state,
    This dim vast vale of tears, vacant and desolate?
    Ask why the sunlight not forever
    Weaves rainbows o'er yon mountain river,
    Why aught should fail and fade that once is shown,
    Why fear and dream and death and birth
    Cast on the daylight of this earth
    Such gloom,—why man has such a scope
    For love and hate, despondency and hope?

NO VOICE from some sublimer world hath ever
To sage or poet these responses given—
Therefore the name of God and ghosts and Heaven,
Remain the records of their vain endeavour,
Frail spells—whose uttered charm might not avail to sever
From all we hear and all we see,
Doubt, chance, and mutability.
Thy light alone—like mist o'er mountains driven, .
Or music by the night wind sent
Through strings of some still instrument,
Or moonlight on a midnight stream,
Gives grace and truth to life's unquiet dream.

LOVE, HOPE, and Self-esteem, like clouds depart
And come, for some uncertain moments lent.
Man were immortal, and omnipotent,
Didst thou, unknown and awful as thou art,
Keep with thy glorious train firm state within his heart.
Thou messenger of sympathies,
That wax and wane in lovers' eyes—
Thou—that to human thought art nourishment,
Like darkness to a dying flame!
Depart not as thy shadow came,
Depart not—lest the grave should be,
Like life and fear, a dark reality.

——— 0 ———

[PERCY BYSSHE SHELLEY]

From THE PRELUDE, BOOK VI

*T*HE IMMEASURABLE height
  Of woods decaying, never to be decayed,
  The stationary blasts of waterfalls,
  And in the narrow rent at every turn
  Winds thwarting winds, bewildered and forlorn,
  The torrents shooting from the clear blue sky,
  The rocks that muttered close upon our ears,
  Black drizzling crags that spake by the way-side
  As if a voice were in them, the sick sight
  And giddy prospects of the raving stream,
  The unfettered clouds and region of the Heavens,
  Tumult and peace, the darkness and the light—
  Were all like workings of one mind, the features
  Of the same face, blossoms upon one tree;
  Characters of the great Apocalypse,
  The types and symbols of Eternity,
  Of first, and last, and midst, and without end.

——— *o* ———

[WILLIAM WORDSWORTH]

Index of First Lines

List of Illustrations

The publishers would like to thank the following for permission to reproduce. Fine Art Photographic Library Ltd. jacket, pp. 2–3, 8–9, 32–3, 84–5; The Turner Collection, Tate Gallery, London pp. 6, 58–9.

List of Authors

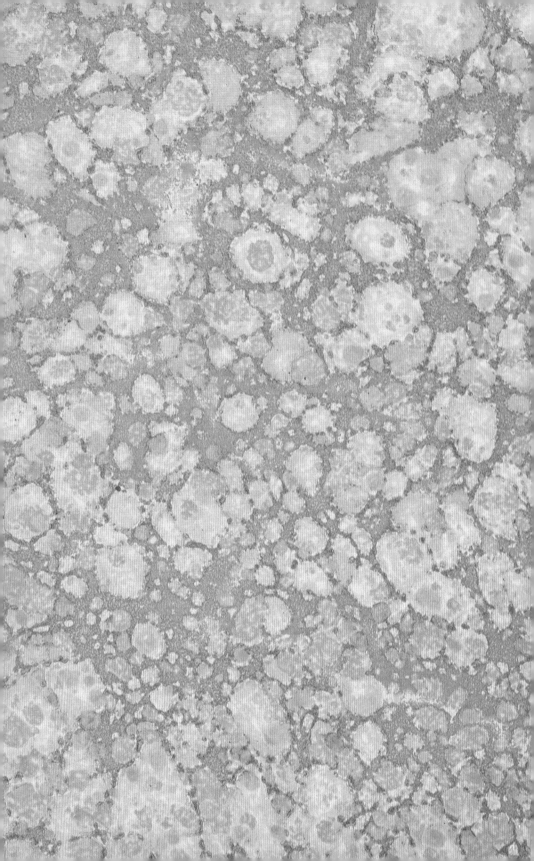